BLUE BANNER
BIOGRAPHY

James
HARDEN

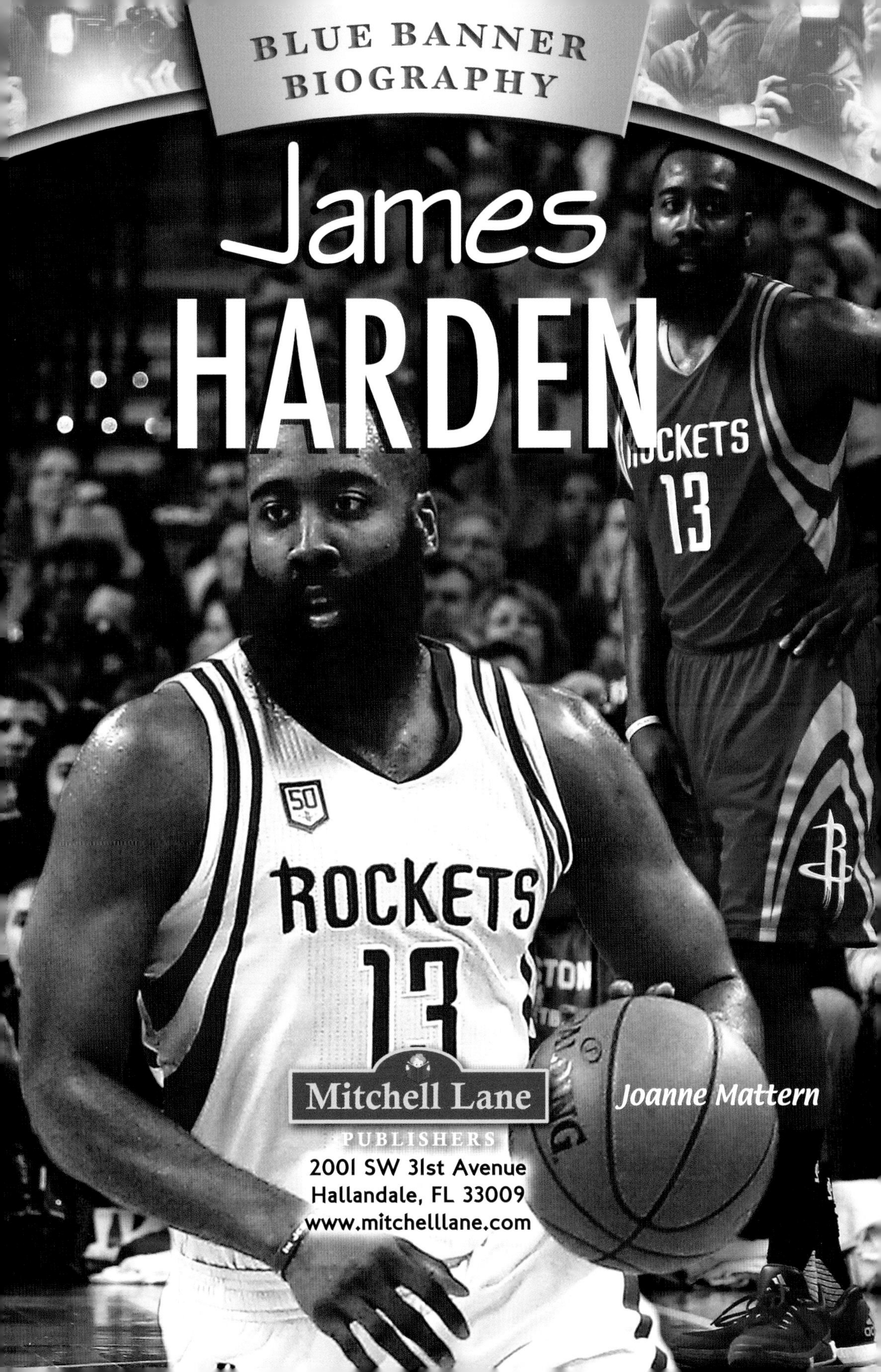

Mitchell Lane
PUBLISHERS
2001 SW 31st Avenue
Hallandale, FL 33009
www.mitchelllane.com

Joanne Mattern

Printing   1   2   3   4   5   6   7   8   9

Blue Banner Biographies

Library of Congress Cataloging-in-Publication Data
Names: Mattern, Joanne, 1963– author.
Title: James Harden / by Joanne Mattern.
Description: Hallandale, FL : Mitchell Lane Publishers, [2018] | Series: Blue banner biographies |
    Includes bibliographical references and index.
Identifiers: LCCN 2017024477 | ISBN 9781680201222 (library bound)
Subjects: LCSH: Harden, James, 1989– —Juvenile literature. | Basketball players—United States—
    Biography—Juvenile literature.
Classification: LCC GV884.H2435 M37 2018 | DDC 796.323092 [B] —dc23
LC record available at https://lccn.loc.gov/2017024477

eBook ISBN: 978-1-68020-123-9

ABOUT THE AUTHOR: Joanne Mattern is the author of many books for children on a variety of subjects, including history and biography. She has written many biographies for Mitchell Lane. Joanne loves to learn about people, places, and events and bring historical figures to life for today's readers. She lives in New York State with her husband, children, and several pets.

PUBLISHER'S NOTE: The following story has been thoroughly researched and to the best of our knowledge represents a true story. While every possible effort has been made to ensure accuracy, the publisher will not assume liability for damages caused by inaccuracies in the data and makes no warranty on the accuracy of the information contained herein. This story has not been authorized or endorsed by James Harden.

Blue Banner Biography

James Harden (13) and his Artesia High School teammates celebrate after winning the 2006 California state championship.

A Reluctant Star

Scott Pera, the basketball coach at California's Artesia High School in southern California, had a problem. His team had just lost its first game of the 2005–06 season against a team from Ohio in a national tournament. On the long plane ride home, Pera walked up the aisle to James Harden. The 16-year-old junior had a lot of promise, but Pera didn't feel that James was living up to his full potential. Pera knew they had to talk.

James was sleeping, but he woke up when Pera sat beside him. The coach did not waste any words. "We can't win unless you start shooting more," he told James.

James looked startled. He thought for a moment. Then he replied, "I don't want everybody to think I'm a gunner." James was afraid his teammates would think he was selfish for taking too many shots.

Pera had already spent many hours working with James, and the teenager had slowly matured into a strong player. But he still was reluctant to dominate on the court.

That night on the plane, Pera had nothing else to say. He went back to his seat and hoped his words had sunk in.

James had to step up his game and realize that the coach and the team wanted him to take more chances.

James tried to go back to sleep, but his coach's words stayed in his head. "We can't win unless you start shooting more." James knew what he had to do. He would start shooting more. Artesia went on to win two state championships. During James's junior and senior years, the team had a 66-3 record.

James's coach was not the only person who was pleased at his change in attitude. His teammates were happy too. "Coming up, he was always the best player,"

James and two Arizona State teammates surround UTEP guard Stefon Jackson during the 76 Classic Tournament in Anaheim, California on November 30, 2008. The Sun Devils won 88–58.

Derek Glasser, who played with James in high school and college, told Grantland.com. "But he never played like he was the best player." It wasn't until Coach Pera's words made James realize that his teammates wanted him to be more competitive on the court that he was able to show his true skills.

James Harden would go on to big things—*very* big things—after high school. Today, even as a star in the National Basketball Association (NBA), he still does not like to be thought of as a ball hog. "I never want anyone to think I'm selfish or anything," he told Grantland.com. "But I usually know when to be aggressive." For James, being aggressive is just one part of why he is such a star.

James's coach was not the only person who was pleased at his change in attitude. His teammates were happy too.

James Harden dribbles the ball up the court during a game against the USC Trojans in 2009.

Learning to Work Hard

James Harden Jr. was born on August 26, 1989, in Los Angeles, California. His father, James Harden Sr. was serving in the U.S. Navy when James was born. After he left the Navy, James Sr. struggled with drugs and was in and out of jail. He did not play a significant role in his son's life as the boy grew up. In turn, James has had little to do with his father as an adult.

James's mother, Monja Willis, worked hard as a customer service representative for AT&T to make a good life for James and his two older siblings. The family lived in a neighborhood that had a lot of crime. Monja's two brothers had been killed in neighborhood violence. She did not want the same thing to happen to her children.

Eventually Monja moved to a neighborhood outside of Los Angeles called Rancho Dominguez. It was much safer and quieter. In fact, the neighborhood was so quiet that the neighbors often complained about James playing basketball in the street.

Growing up, James was a huge basketball fan. He knew, even as a child, that he wanted to play in the NBA.

James Harden hugs his mother, Monja Willis, during a halftime ceremony in 2015 to retire James's Arizona State jersey number. Monja has always been her son's biggest fan.

"He carried around a basketball as if it was his job," James's older brother, Akili Roberson, told *Time* magazine.

James's mother also realized that James had big dreams. "Basketball always has been his first," Monja Willis told the *Houston Chronicle* years later. "When he was in high school, I asked him, 'What do you want to do when you graduate?' He said, 'Mom, I'm going to be an NBA player.' I said, 'No, for real. You have to have an A and a B plan. What's your plan?' 'Mama, my plan is to be an NBA player.'" One day he left a note for her. It read, "Could you leave me a couple of dollars? P.S. Keep this paper. I'm going to be a star."

Physically, James didn't seem like he might be a star. When he enrolled at Artesia, located in nearby Lakewood, he was chubby and suffered from a breathing problem called **asthma**.

He also needed an attitude adjustment. "I just stood in the corner," James told *Sports Illustrated*. "I didn't dribble. I didn't move. I didn't do anything. I was lazy, really lazy." Sometimes he only took eight shots in a game. That was hardly enough to make him stand out.

Pera made James do conditioning exercises every day. The work was hard and tiring. James hated it so much he called it "the worst time of my life." Monja did not want to hear James complain. She knew he had to work hard to achieve his dream. One day, she and James met with Pera. Pera told *Time*, "She looked at him, looked at me, and goes, 'He's the coach, listen to him.'" The complaining stopped. James became a better player.

He also benefited from good timing. Many of the team's top players had graduated the year before. As a result, James got more playing time than Pera normally gave to freshmen. When one of the starting players struggled, James was ready to step in and replace him. He remained a starter for the rest of his high school career.

As a sophomore, James stood 6-4 (en route to his eventual height of 6-5). He averaged 12.3 points per game and helped Artesia finish with a 28-5 record.

It was during his junior year that coach Pera called him out. James responded by averaging close to twenty points per game and leading the team to the state championship.

During the summer of 2006, James played basketball on the **Amateur Athletic Union**'s Pump-N-Run Elite team. At the Super 64 tournament in Las Vegas, he scored 67 points in two games on the same day to lead his team to the title.

As a senior, James played a key role as Artesia won the state championship again. Many authorities ranked the school as number one in the entire country. James was named to the prestigious McDonald's All-American team. Colleges around the country offered him a **scholarship**. James chose Arizona State University in Tempe, Arizona. One of the main reasons was that Pera had taken a job as an assistant coach at the school.

James entered ASU in the fall of 2007. At the time, the Sun Devils were in a slump. The team had finished last in the Pac-10 (now the Pac-12) Conference with a 2-16 mark the previous year.

James's arrival changed all that. From his position as guard, he took charge of the team. The Sun Devils placed fifth in the Pac-10 with a 9-9 record, and were 21-13 overall in the 2007–08 season. James was the team's high scorer with an average of 17.8 points per game. He was named First Team All-Pac-10 and also chosen for the conference All-Freshman Team. The Sun Devils just missed qualifying for the **NCAA Tournament**. Instead, they played in the National Invitational Tournament (NIT). ASU won twice before losing to the Florida Gators.

Around this time, James began sporting a new look. Many people thought he looked younger than he was. James got fed up and decided to make a change. He grew a beard. At first, the beard was small and neat. Later, it became quite bushy. In time, the beard would become an important part of James's image.

James was featured on one of six regional covers of the *Sports Illustrated* 2008 College Basketball Preview issue. By that time, he had become famous at Arizona State. Students began wearing T-shirts that read, "Die Harden Fan." That was a reference to the popular *Die Hard* film series that starred Bruce Willis. He ended the regular season with a 20.1 average and led the Pac-10 in steals. He was voted Pac-10 Player of the Year. The Sun Devils ended the season with a 20-10 record and earned a trip to the 2009 NCAA Tournament.

Unfortunately, James did not do well in the tournament. In the first game against Temple University, he missed most of his shots. Arizona State won anyway. But the Sun Devils lost to Syracuse University in the next round by a score of 78-67. Again, James had a rough game and made only two shots.

Despite his poor performance in the NCAA Tournament, James believed he was ready for the next level. The Syracuse game would be his last as a college player. James announced he would take part in the NBA **draft**.

> James was featured on one of six regional covers of the Sports Illustrated 2008 College Basketball Preview issue. By that time, he had become famous at Arizona State.

NBA Commissioner David Stern shakes hands with a joyous James Harden after James was chosen by the Oklahoma City Thunder in the 2009 NBA draft.

Playing Hard in Oklahoma

On June 25, 2009, the Oklahoma City Thunder chose James as the third overall pick in the draft. The Thunder had moved to Oklahoma City the year before. Previously they had played as the Seattle SuperSonics. James was the first player drafted by the team in their new home.

James had let the Thunder know that he was interested in playing for them. He had worked out with the team a few days before the draft. James also sent a personal letter to Thunder general manager Sam Presti, listing the reasons he wanted to become a part of the team. Presti liked James's talent and attitude.

Being chosen so early put a lot of pressure on James. He knew the fans and everyone on the team expected him to be a star. James wasn't worried. He knew he just had to work hard and earn his spot.

Oklahoma already had two budding superstars, Kevin Durant and Russell Westbrook. So Thunder coach Scott Brooks used James as his sixth man. The sixth man is not a starter, but he is usually the first or second man off the bench. The NBA recognizes the importance of this role. It

James Harden hustles back into the game as Thunder coach Scott Brooks calls out instructions during Game Three of the 2012 NBA Finals. The Miami Heat won the championship, but Harden was praised for his aggressive play.

began the Sixth Man of the Year Award after the 1982–83 season. As a shooting guard, James averaged 9.9 points during his first season with the team.

Fans and NBA officials noticed James's hard work and talent. He was named to the NBA All-Rookie Second Team. More importantly, James helped the Thunder to a 50-32 season. That was a lot better than the 23-59 season they'd had the year before!

Oklahoma City made it to the playoffs, where they faced the top-seeded Los Angeles Lakers. The Thunder won the first two games, but the Lakers won the next four to advance. Even though the Thunder was eliminated, James was a star in all the games.

The 2010-2011 season was another great one for the Thunder and for James. Even though he was just 21 years old, James was one of the most respected players on the team. The Thunder ended the regular season in first place in the Western Conference's Northwest Division and made it to the Western Conference Finals. However, they lost the series to the Dallas Mavericks.

The 2011-2012 season was James's best yet. He won the NBA's Sixth Man of the Year Award. He averaged 16.8

Percy Vaughn of Kia Motors presents James with the Sixth Man of the Year award after the 2011–12 season. Kia is one of the NBA's main sponsors. James led all bench players by averaging nearly 17 points a game.

points per game, and scored 20 or more points 17 times. On April 18, he scored 40 points against the Phoenix Suns. The Thunder swept Dallas in the first round of the playoffs, then beat the Lakers and the San Antonio Spurs to make it to the NBA championships. But the Thunder lost to the Miami Heat, four games to one. James had trouble scoring against Miami's tough defense and hit just seven three-point shots in the five-game series. Miami superstar LeBron James gave James credit for the team's showing. He said, "I think we all know that James Harden was a big part of their team. He was a big part of why they made it to the finals."

During the summer of 2012, James was a member of the U.S. Olympic Team. The U.S. team won the gold medal, though James didn't play much.

When James returned to the United States, he faced a very difficult challenge. The Thunder wanted James to sign a new contract. However, James believed he was one of the best players in the NBA. He wanted more playing time. When James refused to sign the contract, the Thunder traded him to the Houston Rockets.

James was excited for a new opportunity, but he did not want anyone to think he hadn't enjoyed playing for the Thunder. He tweeted, "I would love to thank Oklahoma City for three amazing years!"

The Rockets were thrilled to sign James. "James Harden is a player we can build around, and continue to improve the team around his skills," Rockets general manager Daryl Morey told the media. "He's an underrated player. He's absolutely someone who, when they see him step into the role of a star for the Houston Rockets, people are going to realize just how good he is." A new chapter of James's basketball journey was about to begin.

A Star in Texas

*T*he Houston Rockets were struggling when James joined them in 2012. They had missed the playoffs the past three seasons. James knew he and his $60-million contract would be under a lot of pressure. Miami Heat superstar Dwyane Wade told ESPN, "He can live up to the billing but the grind is tough. Every night to step up to what everyone believes that you should do because of the dollar amount you ask for."

James jumped right into the action. He scored 82 points in his first two games and was named the Western Conference Player of the Week. He received that honor again in early January, averaging more than 29 points that week. He finished the season with career-highs in points, **assists**, **rebounds**, and steals. The Rockets made it to the NBA playoffs but lost to James's old team, the Oklahoma City Thunder, in six games.

The 2013-2014 season was another great one for James. He scored a season-high 43 points in February and helped lead the team to a 54-28 record. Although the Rockets were knocked out in the first round of the playoffs, James was named to the 2014 All-NBA First Team.

James played great on the court, but behind the scenes he was struggling. He had trouble with the role of team leader. "I was being lazy, being tired, wanting to just go home and relax," he explained to *Sports Illustrated*. He also concentrated so hard on offense that he let his defensive play slide.

Once again, James's old coach, Scott Pera, pushed James to change his ways. Pera, now an assistant coach for the Rice Owls team in Houston, visited James. As the two talked about the best players in the NBA, James realized, "The best of the best, they play both ends. I've got to do it too."

James threw himself into hard physical training. He worked on being a leader too. Over the summer, James played for Team USA in the FIBA World Cup. James took on a strong role. "The way he practiced, the way he was in meetings, he's grown quite a bit," one of Team USA's coaches told *Sports Illustrated* as the team won the World Cup.

James agreed. He told NBA.com that leadership is "knowing how to communicate. Knowing how to talk to each player on my team. . . . You've got to approach certain guys certain ways. Show them by working hard. . . . All those things I didn't know in my first two years here. I've been learning and it's paying off."

The 2014-2015 season was another strong one for James, and the Rockets continued their winning ways. Once again Houston made it to the playoffs but was eliminated in the Western Conference championships. The 2015-2016 season started slowly for both James and the Rockets. On January 13, James scored 27 points and reached 10,000 career points. But the Rockets ended with a 41-41 record and were quickly eliminated from the playoffs.

The season also saw trouble between James and his teammate, star player Dwight Howard. The two tried to be friends, but they just did not get along. James thought Howard fooled around too much and was too loud. Howard thought James was too serious and lacked respect. The two could not connect. Howard left the team to play with the Atlanta Hawks. He told ESPN that he was disappointed with how things between him and James

James Harden and his teammate DeMar DeRozan hold the trophy after the U.S. team won the 2014 FIBA World Cup. James scored 23 points as the Americans crushed Serbia 129–92 in the title game.

James (#13) and fellow superstar teammate Dwight Howard (#12) try to work together in the first round of the 2015 Western Conference playoffs. The Rockets defeated the Dallas Mavericks four games to one and eventually played in the Conference Finals. But they lost to Golden State. Howard left the team soon afterward.

worked out. "It wasn't as good as it needed to be for us to succeed. I wish the relationships would have been a lot better."

Things were "a lot better" for James when he signed a new four-year, $118-million contract with the Rockets after the 2015–16 season. James told the media that he planned to stay with the team until the end of his career. "Definitely it's going to end here," he promised. He took his position as the star of the Rockets very seriously. James told the *Houston Chronicle*, "I take it for what it is, try not to get too overwhelmed by it, stay humble, pray about it, just continue to be me. That's all I can be."

A Change for the Better

*H*ouston management was unhappy with the 2015–16 season. So they hired Mike D'Antoni as coach. D'Antoni emphasized an **up-tempo** style of play. He originated it years earlier with the Phoenix Suns, with the motto "Seven seconds or less [to shoot]." That meant pushing the ball down the court as fast as possible and putting up shots from all over the court. The Golden State Warriors adopted the same philosophy in 2014. It resulted in two NBA championships in three years. Warriors coach Steve Kerr told ESPN's J.A. Andade, "Coaches have changed their thinking so you're getting more and more space and open court. . . . And Mike . . . he's the guy who triggered the changes."

D'Antoni didn't fare as well personally. He was fired from several head coaching jobs and was out of basketball entirely when the Rockets hired him. It proved to be a good decision. D'Antoni wanted to make James the centerpiece of the team's offense. He would play point guard and touch the ball on virtually every possession.

At first James thought the new coach was crazy. He would have to learn a new position. But D'Antoni was persuasive. James bought into his approach. So did the rest of the team. Against the New Orleans Pelicans in December, the Rockets set NBA single-game records for three-point shots attempted (61) and made (24). They

James poses with coach Mike D'Antoni during NBA basketball media day on September 23, 2016, in Houston. D'Antoni's style of coaching shook up James and the rest of the team, but led to a great season.

finished with 1,181 three-point shots made, another NBA record. The team's record improved dramatically as well. The Rockets won 55 games, a 14-game improvement. But Houston lost in the second round of the playoffs to San Antonio.

James had his best season. His assists nearly doubled, from an average of 6.5 a game the previous year, to a league-leading 11.2, while scoring 29 points a game. That meant he had a hand in about half of the team's total points. Once again he was All-Pro First Team. For most of the season, James and Westbrook were the leading candidates for the Most Valuable Player Award. James finished a close second. Even better things are in store. "He's learning where to put the furniture, where to put things in his new home," Houston's director of player development John Lucas told *Time*. By "new home" Lucas meant playing point guard. "So we haven't seen the best of him yet."

James is a superstar on the basketball court. He has become a star off the court as well. At first, James found it difficult to be the center of attention. The media and fans watched his every move. They noticed everything, from what brand of sneaker he wore to what he ordered when he went out to dinner. James refused to let the attention change his life. "It comes with it," he explained to the *Houston Chronicle* in 2015. "So I try not to get too overwhelmed. I'm not going to sit there and be in the house and be shackled up. I'm really like a normal guy. I like to do normal things."

One thing that James does like people to pay attention to is his charity work. He supports a number of different charities. Along with other members of the Rockets, he goes on shopping sprees for needy children during every holiday season. James also supports the Special Olympics and breast cancer charities. One of his favorite charities is

James drives to the basket in a game against his former Oklahoma City teammates on January 5, 2017. He scored 26 points as the Rockets recorded a 118–116 victory.

the Jeremy Lin Foundation, started by his former Rockets teammate and good friend. The Foundation's goal is to "love and serve children and youth by providing hope, empowerment, and leadership development."

James's mother manages his charity work. She is still amazed at what her son has accomplished. "My eyes still get big with it all," she told the *Houston Chronicle*. "I'm still in awe. This is really my son."

James tries to take his celebrity and his basketball feats in stride. He knows he is blessed. "I think all of it is cool," he told the *Chronicle*. "There's no way, shape, or form that I should be moping around at all. . . . Everything is in a good place right now. I'm smiling and just riding the wave." For James and his fans, it's been a wonderful ride.

James enjoys charity work, especially working with children. Here James gives his shoes to cancer patient Patrick DeClaire and his twin brother, Trent, after a game against the Sacramento Kings.

CHRONOLOGY

1989	James Edwards Harden Jr. is born in Los Angeles on August 26.
2003–2007	James plays for Artesia High School in California.
2007–2009	James plays for Arizona State University.
2009	James is chosen by the Oklahoma City Thunder as the third overall pick in the NBA draft.
2009–2012	James plays for the Thunder.
2012	James is traded to the Houston Rockets; he plays on the U.S. Olympic team.
2014	James is named to the NBA All-Pro First Team; he plays on Team USA in the FIBA World Cup.
2016	James signs a $118 million contract with the Rockets.
2017	James finishes a close second in voting for the NBA's Most Valuable Player.

CAREER STATS

Season	Team	GP	GS	PPG	RPG	APG	SPG
2009-10	OK City	76	0	9.9	3.2	1.8	1.1
2010-11	OK City	82	5	12.2	3.1	2.1	1.1
2011-12	OK City	62	2	16.8	4.1	3.7	1.0
2012-13	Houston	78	78	25.9	4.9	5.8	1.8
2013–14	Houston	73	73	25.4	4.7	6.1	1.6
2014-15	Houston	81	81	27.4	5.7	7.0	1.9
2015-16	Houston	82	82	29.0	6.1	6.5	1.7
2016-17	Houston	81	81	29.1	8.1	11.2	1.5
Career		615	402	22.1	5.0	5.7	1.5

Legend: G = games played, GS = games started, PPG = points per game, RPG = rebounds per game, APG = assists per game, SPG = steals per game
Source: http://www.espn.com/nba/player/stats/_/id/3992/james-harden

GLOSSARY

Amateur Athletic Union (AM-uh-chur ath-LET-ik YOON-yuhn)—organization dedicated to promoting amateur sports and physical fitness in the United States

assists (uh-SISTS)—passes to teammates that result in them scoring a basket

asthma (AZTH-muh)—lung spasms that cause difficulty in breathing

draft (DRAFT)—annual selection of players by NBA teams

NCAA Tournament (ehn-see-A-A TUHR-nuh-muhnt)—annual tournament of the country's top basketball teams; often called March Madness

rebounds (REE-boundz)—controlling the ball after a missed shot

scholarship (SKAHL-uhr-ship)—payment to a student to help with his or her education, usually based on need, athletic ability, or accomplishments in school

up-tempo (up-TEHM-poe)—playing at a high rate of speed

FURTHER READING

Books

Fishman, Jon M. *James Harden*. Minneapolis: Lerner Publications, 2016.

Redban, Bill. *James Harden: The Inspirational Story of Basketball Superstar James Harden*. Seattle, WA: CreateSpace Independent Publishing Platform, 2014.

On the Internet

James Harden–Biography
   http://www.jockbio.com/Bios/J_Harden/J_Harden_bio.html

James Harden Stats
   http://www.basketball-reference.com/players/h/hardeja01.html

James Harden Stats, Details, Videos, and News
   http://www.nba.com/players/james/harden/201935

Jeremy Lin Foundation
   http://www.jeremylinfoundation.org/

Works Consulted

Adler, Lindsey. "James Harden Says Last Year Was the Worst of His Life." http://deadspin.com/james-harden-says-last-year-was-the-worst-of-his-life-1792893542

Andande, J.A. "Suns, D'Antoni influence on the NBA Finals." ESPN, June 5, 2015. http://www.espn.com/nba/playoffs/2015/story/_/id/13023943/nba-playoffs-phoenix-suns-mike-dantoni-influence-nba-finals

Arritt, Dan. "Artesia Junior Has Grown into Game." *Los Angeles Times*, March 11, 2006. http://articles.latimes.com/2006/mar/11/sports/sp-hsharden11

Blinebury, Fran. "Harden: 'I am the MVP.'" nba.com, April 9, 2015. http://www.nba.com/2015/news/features/fran_blinebury/04/09/harden-declares-he-is-this-years-mvp/

Conn, Jordan Ritter. "The Many Faces of James Harden." May 29, 2012. Grantland.com. http://grantland.com/features/the-many-faces-oklahoma-city-thunder-guard-james-harden/

FURTHER READING

Duncan, Chris. "Rockets Land 'Foundational Player' in James Harden. Associated Press, October 29, 2012. http://www.csnmidatlantic.com/rockets-land-foundational-player-james-harden?amp

Feigen, Jonathan. "James Harden: Rising Star On and Off the Court." *Houston Chronicle*, October 15, 2015. http://www.houstonchronicle.com/sports/rockets/article/James-Harden-Rising-star-on-and-off-the-court-657

Gregory, Sean. "To Rule the NBA, James Harden Needed to Embrace Letting Go." *Time*, February 16, 2017. http://time.com/4672996/james-harden-rule-nba/

Herbert, James. "Report: Dwight Howard Frustrated at Lack of Respect from James Harden." CBS Sports, April 27, 2016. http://www.cbssports.com/nba/news/report-dwight-howard-frustrated-at-lack-of-respect-from-james-harden

Jenkins, Lee. "A Simple Plan." *Sports Illustrated*, March 6, 2017, pp. 36–43.

Jenkins, Lee. "James Harden, the NBA's Unlikely MVP." *Sports Illustrated*, February 18, 2015. http://www.si.com/nba/2015/02/18/james-harden-houston-rockets-mvp-midseason-report

Joseph, Andrew. "Dwight Howard on James Harden: 'I Wish the Relationship Would Have Been a Lot Better.'" *USA Today*, July 14, 2016. http://ftw.usatoday.com/2016/07/dwight-howard-james-harden-relationship-rockets-hawks-nba

Tramel, Berry. "What They Are Saying About the James Harden Trade." *NewsOk*, October 28, 2012. http://newsok.com/article/3723513

INDEX